JOHN THOMPSON'S
EASIEST PIANO COURSE

FIRST CHRISTMAS HITS

CONTENTS

ISBN 978-1-4803-9368-4

WILLIS MUSIC

Exclusively Distributed By

HAL•LEONARD®
CORPORATION
7777 W. BLUEMOUND RD. P.O. BOX 13819
MILWAUKEE, WISCONSIN 53213

Visit Hal Leonard Online at
www.halleonard.com

Where Are You Christmas?

from DR. SEUSS' HOW THE GRINCH STOLE CHRISTMAS

Words and Music by Will Jennings,
James Horner and Mariah Carey
Arranged by Carolyn Miller

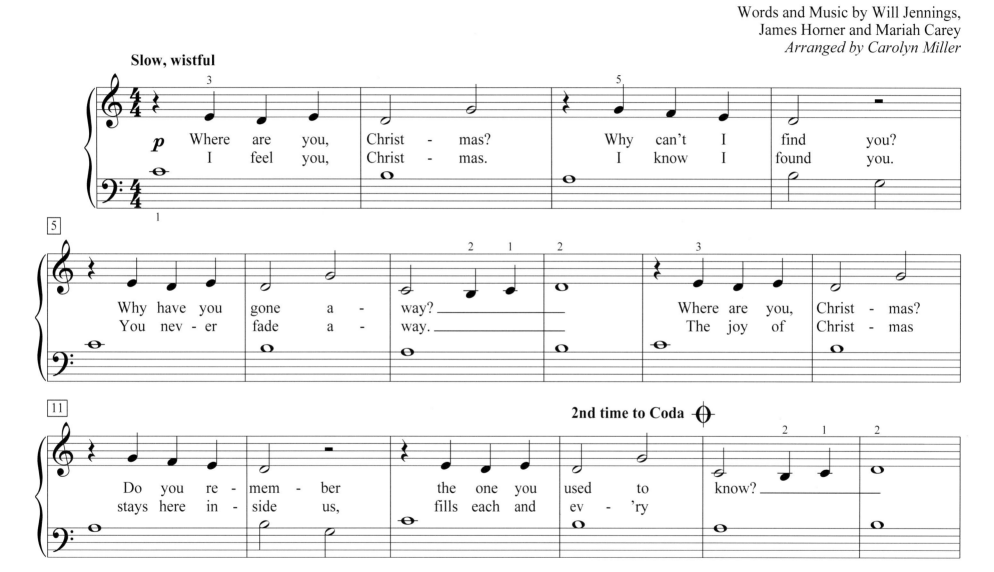

[]

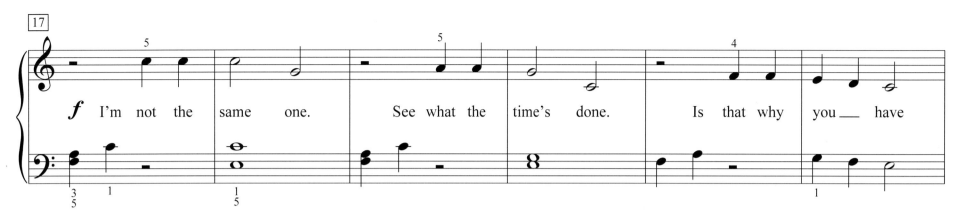

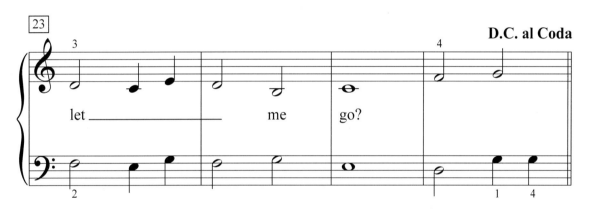

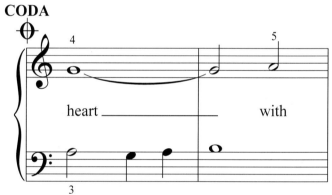

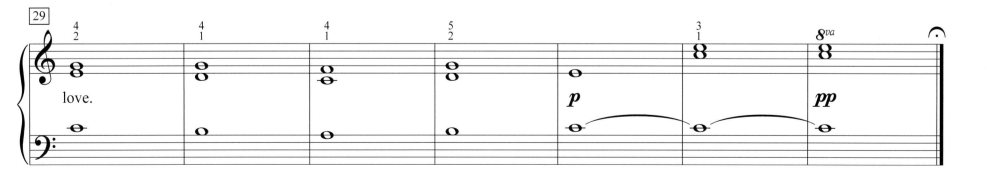

Mister Santa

Words and Music by Pat Ballard
Arranged by Carolyn Miller

4

Somewhere in My Memory

from the Twentieth Century Fox Motion Picture HOME ALONE

Words by Leslie Bricusse
Music by John Williams
Arranged by Carolyn Miller

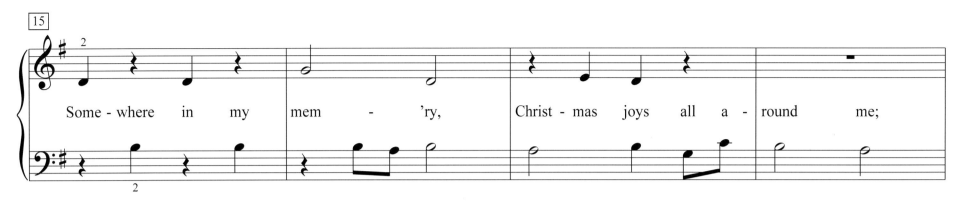

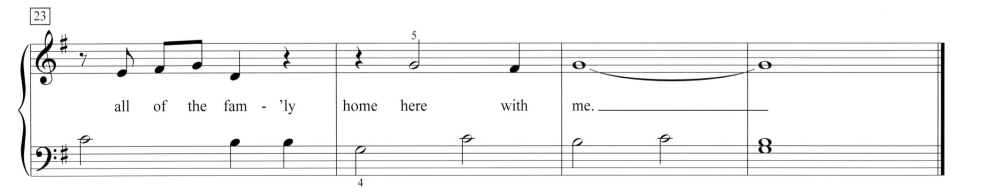

A Holly Jolly Christmas

Music and Lyrics by Johnny Marks
Arranged by Carolyn Miller

9

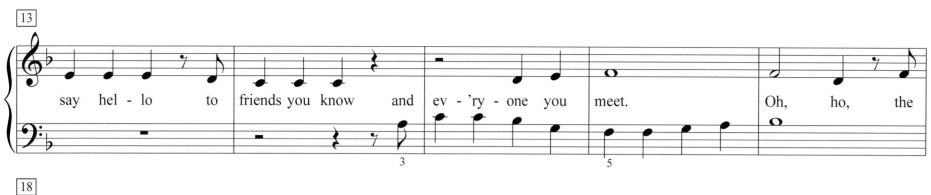

say hel - lo to friends you know and ev - 'ry - one you meet. Oh, ho, the

mis - tle - toe hung where you can see. Some - bod - y waits for you, kiss her once for

me. Have a hol - ly jol - ly Christ-mas, and in case you did - n't hear,

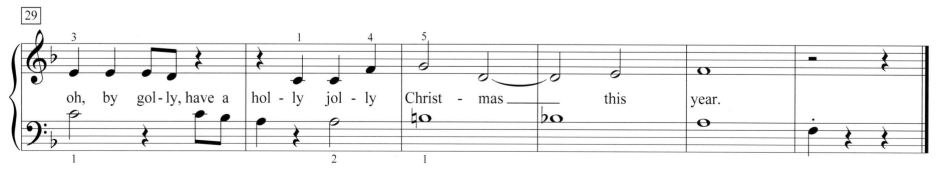

oh, by gol - ly, have a hol - ly jol - ly Christ - mas this year.

All I Want for Christmas Is My Two Front Teeth

Words and Music by Don Gardner
Arranged by Carolyn Miller

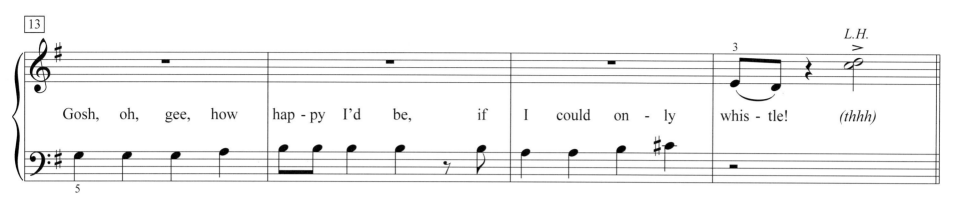

Gosh, oh, gee, how hap-py I'd be, if I could on-ly whis-tle! *(thhh)*

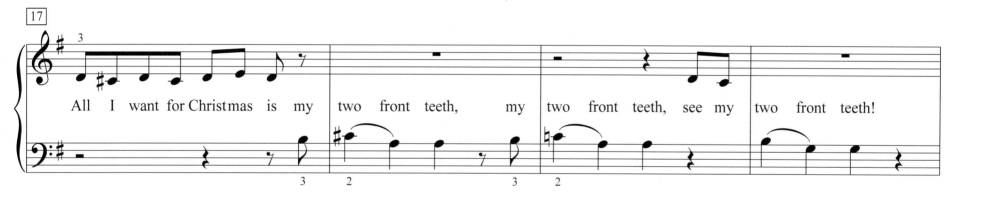

All I want for Christmas is my two front teeth, my two front teeth, see my two front teeth!

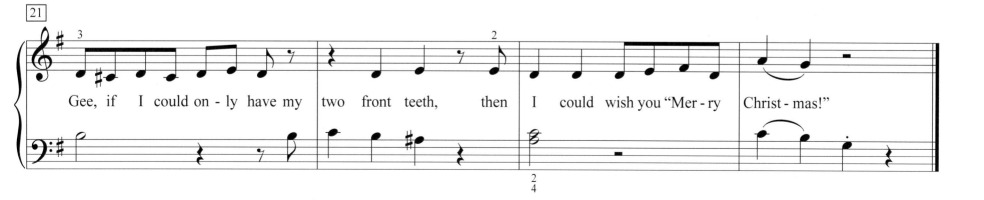

Gee, if I could on-ly have my two front teeth, then I could wish you "Mer-ry Christ-mas!"

Grandma Got Run Over by a Reindeer

Words and Music by Randy Brooks
Arranged by Carolyn Miller

The Chipmunk Song

Words and Music by Ross Bagdasarian
Arranged by Carolyn Miller

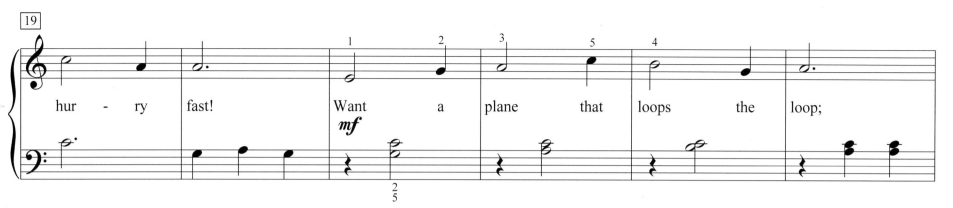

hur - ry fast! Want a plane that loops the loop;

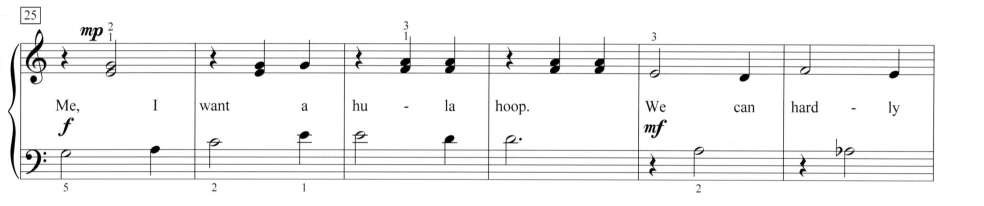

Me, I want a hu - la hoop. We can hard - ly

stand the wait. Please, Christ - mas, don't be late.

Feliz Navidad

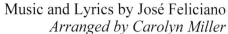

Music and Lyrics by José Feliciano
Arranged by Carolyn Miller